The Mouth Is Also a Compass

Carrie Bennett

©2024 by Carrie Bennett
All rights reserved

Cover Art: Ari Kwon
Cover Design: Catherine Charbonneau
Interior Design: Michelle Caraccia

Published 2024 by Barrow Street, Inc.
(501) (c) (3) corporation. All contributions are tax deductible.
Distributed by:
    Barrow Street Books
    c/o University of Rhode Island
    English Department, Swan 114
    60 Upper College Road
    Kingston, RI 02881

Barrow Street Books are also distributed by Itasca Books Distribution & Fulfillment, 210 Edge Place, Minneapolis MN, 55418, itascabooks.com. Telephone (844) 488-4477; amazon.com; Ingram Periodicals Inc., 1240 Heil Quaker Blvd, PO Box 7000, La Vergne, TN 37086-700 (615) 213-3574; and Armadillo & Co., 7310 S. La Cienega Blvd, Inglewood, CA 90302, (310) 693-6061.

Special thanks to the University of Rhode Island English Department and especially the PhD Program in English, 60 Upper College Road, Swan 114, Kingston, RI 02881, (401) 874-5931, which provides valuable in-kind support, including graduate and undergraduate interns.

First Edition

Library of Congress Control Number: 2024943695

ISBN: 978-1-962131-04-9

The Mouth Is Also a Compass
Carrie Bennett

Barrow Street Press
New York City

CONTENTS

To Break Open a Sea
    The Expedition Begins   1
    The Evidence Escaped Like Smoke   2
    The Accident   3
    Every Field Contains a Frozen Bird   4
    Days North of Me   5
    Up Singing Late Alternatives   6
    Dreaming Inside a Glacier   7
    The Ice Hospital   8
    Sunrise Meets Sunset   9
    Arctic Isolation 1   10
    Solitude Is a Wolf   11
    Arctic Isolation 2   12
    Wristwatch Nostalgia   13
    When Time Becomes a Tunnel   14
    Up Singing Late Regret   15
    Arctic Isolation 3   16
    The Animals Begin to Gather   17
    Up Singing Late Yesterday   18
    My Mouth Is a Compass   19
    A Woman Can Be a Wolf   20

Fragments Inside the Storm   25

The Explorer's Handbook of Survival
    Chapter 1: [How to Survive Subzero Temperatures] 43
    Chapter 2: [How to Handle a Wounded Animal] 44
    Chapter 3: [How to Survive the Long Night] 47
    Chapter 4: [How to Capture Light] 48
    Chapter 5: [How to Survive Common Diseases] 49
    Chapter 6: [How to Abandon Loneliness] 51
    Chapter 7: [How to Forget Snow] 52
    Chapter 8: [How to Survive a Rising Sea] 53
    Chapter 9: [How to Baffle the Wind] 54
    Chapter 10: [How to Embrace the Rubble] 55
    Chapter 11: [How to Greet the End] 56
    Chapter 12: [How a Species Becomes Extinct] 57
    Chapter 13: [How to Dream of the Last Ice Age] 58
    Chapter 14: [How to Find the Last Ice Age] 59
    Chapter 15: [How to Locate a Trapdoor] 60
    Chapter 16: [How the Last Ice Age Appears] 61

Notes
Acknowledgments

"In the first light of dawn, a black cloud grew from the sea. They saw the shape of the storm coming towards them, taking up the whole sky."
—Megan Hunter, *The End We Start From*

"You have to be fatalistic. It's the only way to survive."
—Yto Barrada

To Break Open a Sea

The Expedition Begins

Before I leave, Fifth Avenue becomes a desert. The work is done. I need more solitude to uncover the auroral work caught up in the waves. The weather is personal. Robots observe the earth, clouds scrape the horizon. Machines on every island, the coast fixed like a brainstem to chart destruction. My inadequacies crowd the night. A throwing bridge, a heaving ocean. Below broken ice, a hurricane-whipped water frozen at the height of blow. The unbroken night lasts eight months. A city or a raft, a sunless wastewater. Lost creatures ambush my ship. I leave to find the Last Ice Age.

The Evidence Escaped Like Smoke

At least I haven't lost the moon—

after the fires and floods and droughts,

after the flocks of birds fell to land.

Now I crave a sky the color of peaches.

I crave warm water with lemon.

My real luxury, still starlight.

My eyes keep cowling to men

who either serve authority

or tomorrow. No beleaguered

sea ever defends the law.

It is mapped out in either direction:

blotting out barriers, bottomless

blocks of history. See nothing, blank.

I'm careful, lost like a distant sail.

The Accident

I fall down a crater. This is bad, very bad. I survive the cracked door. Freeze an ear, still weak. The shattered ladder is leaf-like, I shrink in the minute. At times the sky is scattered petals. Think pink anemones, reflections, a forest fire. My world requires a telescope, confidence, stars, and invention. A very dark sunrise. I try two frequencies: shadowless, cloud-marred. The gloomy evenness is almost gone. OK here. OK, OK, OK. Mint-julep crystals and camping gear. The journey is sharp, dangerous. Can almost see a trapdoor. Hours, then silence. I feel bound. To what?

Every Field Contains a Frozen Bird

Not even a footprint left
behind. Maps scatter like soft
stars through fields.
Where are the scientists
that charted this land?
Bright flags wave and I close
my eyes to a sky filled
with songbirds I'll never see
again. My backyard cut
with yellow, a sharp streak
of blue. Will I forget
the red beak of a cardinal?
Sometimes I see phantoms—
strands of smoke or breath
or sprays of white flowers.
I stand for hours in front
of fallen rocks. I am grateful
for the wolf following me.

Days North of Me

I bend close to the ground,

learn to name objects by feel.

Before me a dry valley filled

with sea-spoiled leaves the color

of steel. Certain shallow ice

shelves mean betrayal.

Ringed water means callousness,

refusal. Some moss is soft

as fur but I know better

than to fall asleep.

After thunderstorms clouds

turn to stone. Weird weather

hovers like a sticky fog. I learn

to half sleep standing up.

I strap soft bags of water on my

back like the last woman alive.

Up Singing Late Alternatives

As if my mouth was the little clear covering. As if a well wildly filled the flashlight on my wrist. As if sinking seaworthiness nailed the tallest tree. As if fire, my hands drank a number of small stones. As if clocks ticked confident in escape. As if stronger nourishment: a piece of chocolate, later whatever twisted on the floor still warm. Write a message to the Last Ice Age: reasons for weak fire, unbearable breath. As if a shelter so friendly seemed mistaken. As if sleeping pills, cupped palm, shrinking universe. As if call it God. I learn snow means a gallon more. I learn night means a condition reporting. As if my words would betray me. Suffer salt crackers, unspeakable night, magnificent, I had, I had light. As if these were facts. But how? You precious cobweb by the shelf. As if. As if poor thing haunted too.

Dreaming Inside a Glacier

I run until I see a shining sign
with a map to an ice hospital.
Each time I reach the sign,
it fades farther into the distance
like a metal mirage. I paint
my eyelids into bright finches.
I try to trick the sky
and the machines above
the clouds. Across a river
floats an enormous marble
head with missing eyes.
A single chair stands
on the riverbank. When I sit
my hands turn to paper boats.
The sun sets like wingless birds.

The Ice Hospital

The wolf is my shadow, I feel
her sharp movement.

Cloud patterns spread slowly
across the windowed walls

like a moving lake. The hospital
rooms are terrible elevators

the wolf and I move through.
Everyone in this new city

lives on tubes attached
to their stomachs, a thick

off-white formula pushes
through their bodies.

Their hands reach as I walk
out the door. I search for food

but the stores are coffins.

Sunrise Meets Sunset

I attempt contact with the Last Ice Age. Switches and coils my heart misgives the Morse code. Spend hours melting snow over the weak spots. I'm caught now. Really caught, double-action and all. Ice alone was not to blame. Yesterday's failures impress me, emergencies already planned. Thirty-five feet below, I know a hard brittle. I know bitterness evaporates what washes up. I can walk, I can't leave nice straight lines. Unpredictable nakedness, I rarely spend time forgetting civilization. I will remember microscopic touch like firecrackers, coats, every exposed object. At home I used to trace the glow thrown up. Like a little watchtower, I spent evenings stowed behind locked doors, blinds tight as lids. Barely a streak of light, too busy, too tired. I drove my car, ate my meals, bought my clothes. Ground to a sinking, the ocean forced to hold my abundant weaknesses. Could almost ignore the next storm in the blazing newness of each morning. Now I dig a hole collecting the windvane. A fearful lifting remains, the lowest pin. Contrive a cure to cut so much. Huge red barrier edge. This latitude itself free. All innocently water, water, still more water.

Arctic Isolation 1

My only companion,
the wolf of course.

She pushes her nose
to air and everything

unseen. Wanders away,
later finds me by fire.

Lowers her head
to my lap. We sit

like that for a long time.
When I open my eyes

she is next to me
under a blanket

hardened by ice.
All night she tried

to hide a bone under
my hand. Her nose

raw and bleeding.
Why didn't I wake up?

Solitude Is a Wolf

Good luck mistake, I break the fire. Underground a task sometimes sounds soundless. My self surfaces, unsettles into another planetary memory. Was wrong about the ache. Was wrong felt fine. The only fault was censorship which did not recognize me without a falcon, a spent rocket, a simple tool. Light crystals big as a shadow box, moonlit apple-green. Suppose the disorder is breath's freezing mittens. Also the wolf. In civilization more of a wrench in me clocked the air. Absent-minded galaxies, my animal-escape clears the clouds for a momentary revelation. Not enough to carry regret, a boulder between shoulder blades. I try to teach the wolf not to trust men.

Arctic Isolation 2

Memories live
on moving snowdrifts—

a clock bell echoing
in darkness. Or car

horns, a conversation
muted by rain, an airplane

overhead. The buzz
of a single bee.

A background of steady
machines thrumming.

The sharp horizon line.
How it bleeds

from orange to red to pink.
How the sky slowly

turns off like a cave
of forgetting or falling

over a bottomless cliff.

Wristwatch Nostalgia

Now darkness means throat,

a trapdoor to surrender

craving. In my small hollow

a few inches of edible leaves,

their dried bodies folded

into brittle wings. I collect

poisonous plants to preserve

what little food is left.

All winter I catch myself

looking at my wrist.

From my jacket pocket

I make orange flags.

Leave them hanging

along the cold rock

walls as I push farther

into the next breaking.

When Time Becomes a Tunnel

Yesterday a yellow blur of *if*,
dawnlight fades whitely.
I can define a hard sky:
for warmth brought a blizzard.
O searchlight of scrap metal,
remember I have no radio.
Whose chemicals to clear?
Weather report, balloon soundings,
another cold cranking.
A tunnel by the lantern's
light. I hear a voice. Yes you
by the ice crystals. Be careful,
the weather is dying.

Up Singing Late Regret

My better broken vanished, my fingers uncontrollable. My sometimes did a flight reflect. My *why bother?* Pretty silly afterward, you otherwise. You weak hold, you greatest enemy. I write lungs, my minor misfortune, my yellowed places. Mostly my existence, little, little. Lantern, it's a tough job this stupor. My trace a map north. Could have been more careful with the Last Ice Age. Even now I sometimes. How fingers won't obey. *You stop, you stop.* I'm trying A, B, C, my three mouthfuls of meteoric snow. I am transparent turret, four quadrants in a cave. It's not over yet trapdoor. As though a great city of draining light. Bright weathervane, try the words *peace, tempt.*

Arctic Isolation 3

The wolf mothers me.
She cleans my face,

my palms, her tongue
and eyes the color

of amber. We sit
as close to the fire

as we can. No plan,
I look everywhere

for the outlines
of other planets.

The Animals Begin to Gather

I sit in the wreckage until I can't

see my hands. Until I scramble

the impulse to cover my eyes.

A broken building's entrance

stands like a forgotten mouth.

I find a fallen berry with light-

green skin some bird has emptied

out. A trumpet-throated field

mouse sits next to a single tree.

A bear watches me, its claws

like hooks or shells. Near my wrist

a felt-tipped monarch lands.

Image is both real and hollow.

Up Singing Late Yesterday

If outside my window a robin's rusted chest. If I stood to watch it eat red berries. If holly bush and piece of sun on my arm. If in the distance winter branches bare as arrows. If windproof room with yellow walls. If couch, a lamp for light, if books to read. If dog curled next to me. If single orchid, petals pink like tongue. If comfort meant breath an easy place to settle. If hope opened to throat, a mute wish dislodged. If any moment could return to a wandering tide.

My Mouth Is a Compass

I prepare to leave
my vanishing glacier.

All morning cracked
moth patterns

spread on ice.
I try to keep

the water warm
to wash my hands.

The bear circles
my shelter. The sky

a wide burial above.
Please forgive me.

I follow the purple trace
of a hurricane on the roof.

I close my eyes
to witness disasters.

A Woman Can Be a Wolf

I carve an outline of my body

on layers of ice. Cracks appear

from chest to wrist. My face sinks

farther beneath the surface.

I try to make my mind blank,

unfold myself one body part

at a time. It is better this way.

A city has followed me

like a dream that turns.

I wait for the wolf to find me.

Fragments Inside the Storm

    my eyes crouch
            to the sockets

                      watch the ground
          to see what
shape

the snowdrifts wish
                to take

\+ + +

                my hope
      is a waiting

                        solar system

              swarming
     with stars

                      the weather
          might
be mending

\+ + +

how far can I go
       with this storm—

              carve a thin line
              into the ground
     to record
my existence

\+ + +

my new rule:

      I will punish
           myself if I

    damage a tree
or shrub
         or any living
thing even
  if
       by accident

+ + +

buildings
    stand like
crumbling caves

        clouds hover
     a single strain
     of white cells

+ + +

makeshift landscape
        a collapse

stalled
    to raft

of flinching
      blindness

\+ + +

        up all night
rearranging the Last
              Ice Age

\+ + +

        lost view

in my mind—

                American
      beech

sweet
birch
      stunted
            aspen
     ash
         red
oak
      bright colony
of
      bluestem
            berry bushes
and wild roses

+ + +

                of clocks sure
memory
       of disaster
so simple
             of little nevertheless
     down my chest—

to hole the hurt with me

+ + +

             blame recognized
    the blow
    at fault

+ + +

my iceberg
        sings
unseen
        melting

                to a
sea
        startled
green

+ + +

above
        me
a
burning
        house
                without
        walls
                more
currents
        circle

like a lost
                creature

+ + +

other items to understand:

a ripped bag
      thinness
weakest ship

                purple lilacs
          the smallest
              helmets

dead sparrow
      a chalky
resistance

                rusted wheel
         residue dry
            pollen

broken ladder
      splinter-stuck
finger-split

            rows of
        twisted
            steel beams

+ + +

                  fog rolls
          on forever
                    without
        fear

\+ + +

    sometimes I speak
          and my words
                    sound red

\+ + +

        other languages
        awaken

                dawn beyond
the barrier wastes

                        sea light ebbs
          in longitudes

\+ + +

trapdoor
        my lungs
sliding
little throat

I couldn't be
            the ladder

      of something
      else

\+ + +

the mouth
wasn't

                strong enough
      to grow
                    a hyacinth

\+ + +

        no moon
tonight
            clouds like
      coughs
in my
          pinprick
     chest

\+ + +

another piece
     of hunger
grew
   there

+ + +

                my fingers
        sprout yellow

dust
        to seed

and a single
speckled feather
                    inside
            my pocket

+ + +

the evidence
        disappears
like pollen

\+ + +

memory
        is a reverse
                      hurricane
            no entry could

summon all
        the dead

\+ + +

underwater
        landslide

                cleaved
        iceberg
bright like
                stained glass

a carousel
        moves beneath

        me waiting
to wake
        up

\+ + +

what I know:
        the trapdoor

won't bloom
                and wolf
is a language

        that answers only
                to speed
        and freedom

\+ + +

my sole
        resistance
                    clock prey

            a shrinking
                moon
back
        from the
        blizzard

pebbles
        for ears

+ + +

call it
                  next day
        call it
ray of coronas
                    my heart
            a sinking
                          ship

+ + +

in the dream I hide
            all the
      animals
      in a deep hole

hope will keep
            them safe
      until
      morning

The Explorer's Handbook of Survival

Chapter 1:
[How to Survive Subzero Temperatures]

Remember that you come from deer, that your hands were once hooves, that you ate only green, that you lifted your head and saw a rifle, that you lifted your head and saw white frost-flowers veining the ground, that your body was all movement.

Now a dragonfly lives in your mouth.

Now you must collect large rocks to make a circle.

Now you must sit inside the rock circle all day as the cold accumulates.

Place your burden here.

Chapter 2:
[How to Handle a Wounded Animal]

You are responsible for recovering every wounded animal.

If the wounded animal breathes as though it were underwater, in terrible gulps or sharp pants, make a humming noise.

If the wounded animal makes a chirping or clicking sound, a stammer, a thump, if its body heaves up and down as though a pump moves inside its stomach, if its whiskers and lips twitch, a tick like a switch, if its big paws paddle the air, if it bares its teeth, let it sleep.

Your presence may comfort.

Even if the wounded animal runs from you, even if it is shot in the critical heart-lung, even if you mark in your mind the spot it has fallen, in cover, watch over it.

Crows and ravens may lead you back to the wounded animal.

Stay at a safe distance. A wounded animal will attack its own cubs.

If the wounded animal's eyes are bloodshot, if they weep rusty water or are frozen in a stare, if they wildly blink or stutter or seem to stumble inside their sockets, build a fire.

If the wounded animal is bleeding from its eyes, look up at the sky.

If the wounded animal's body suddenly seizes, is stripped of suppleness, if its chest is strapped by some unseen and terrible belt, place a swatch of soft fabric over its rigid and rippling body.

If the wounded animal has hidden under pine needles, broken bark or fallen logs, stand still without making a sound.

If there is no slight breath, no small sigh or struggle, no wheezing or wobbly exhale, no hollowed-out moan, no low groan or lonely murmur, if there is nothing left of the wounded animal, place your hand on its head.

There is no God to hear your prayer.

Kneel and press your forehead into the earth. Do you hear the wind push through the dry grass?

At least there is that.

At least there is the sky with its burning colors.

If you fail your wounded animal, if you went looking for water or food or shelter, if you let your hunger distract you, if night fell before you could dress its wounds or bathe its broken leg, if you forgot the exact diameter surrounding the wounded animal, the contours of ash field and ice-covered stream, or crumbling mountain and wide pasture, you are still responsible. You are still responsible even at night, even in the darkness of your tent, even in your sleep, even in your sleep.

Chapter 3:
[How to Survive the Long Night]

Learn to live on air. At altitudes over thirty thousand feet the blood thins to hypodermic needles, the breath becomes a rusted pump that continues its mechanical rise and fall. The body keeps going like a line of burnt grass that extends to whatever cliff waits ahead. Forward, forward. The path straight, then not straight. At altitudes of fifty-two thousand feet strange birds call down from tall rocks. All the trees are ash. Lightning sharp as metal splits the cloud banks. Then sun, moon, sky turn to cave.

Chapter 4:
[How to Capture Light]

Learn the old ways of illumination. Candles burn thick and heavy in any temporary shelter hooked to the side of a mountain. You hang there, a precarious cocoon. If you fall, you fall.

Chapter 5:
[How to Survive Common Diseases]

LOST FOG

Lost fog can occur when atmospheric pressures in the body mirror that of the environment. Locating fire-mirrors, blanket-shelters, or heavy matchsticks will prevent fog from entering through the mouth.

GROUND THIRST

A condition when the tongue becomes branched. Hollowed-out cards and collapsible alarms may alleviate thirst.

BONE HUNGER

When the body burrows too deeply inside itself, fling-knives, neck-knives, and rubble-knives are required to extricate loneliness.

BURIED THROAT

Buried throat disease may appear after exposure to contaminated dirt. A fallow nest of filters and a packet of seeds will help counteract this condition.

WOLF ENVY

On any given trail there is yearning. Using a lightening road map will help illuminate an opened mouth.

BIRCH SADNESS

A body is also a tree. O bruised chest bundle. O little trapdoor of throwing feathers. Recall a moment of flight to release breath.

Chapter 6:
[How to Abandon Loneliness]

Don't be sentimental about walking under a cluster of white lilacs one evening in spring. How the sun faded so carefully even the birds forgot to stop singing. Don't think about your mouth, how you easily swallowed sweetness. Now you know that any abyss shines starkly. As if nothing could ever be nothing again.

Chapter 7:
[How to Forget Snow]

Forget winters when all you know is snow. Endless falling to muted piles high as humans. Forget walking through cold tunnels, warm breath smeared in bitter air, plows a processional of spewing salt and sand. Forget snow days. Forget skating, sledding. Forget children making snowballs.

When the warmer winters arrive, you have December picnics, abandon your scarf in a basement bin. You glow in your good fortune, how lucky to leave your boots behind.

Eventually you forget the word for snow, for a pink post-blizzard sky, sharp echo of fallen icicles, windows etched with frost feathers. You forget shock of brightness, trees shedding glitter everywhere, slanted shadows edging across a speechless street.

Chapter 8:
[How to Survive a Rising Sea]

Remember that you come from the sea. Thirty-five thousand feet beneath, any creature absorbs a darkness complete. The seafloor expands to a new roundness. O confused moon. O single cell soft as tongue. At these depths division is a different dawn mute and searching.

Chapter 9:
[How to Baffle the Wind]

Encase the ground in mirrors to reflect the moving clouds back to sky. Migrating birds circle the same field until they fall asleep mid-flight. Eventually a garden of strawberries the color of quartz swells into a pale kaleidoscope of leaf and petal. Buried deep beneath the dirt a pair of lungs expands into a lullaby to hold off a hurricane.

Chapter 10:
[How to Embrace the Rubble]

Sing as a city of draining light spins inside a hurricane. There is no broadening twilight, no frost-breath, no sheer beauty, no God. No waves and radio, no adjusted receiver, no trail and thunder. No nail to the floor, no ghost of alternative view. No killing time, no kite or kite signal. No two o'clock, no knees knocking and blur. No flashlight, ladder, broadcast. No blind urging or line-blurred light. No fire fallen, no red traces of flight, no where are they now? No else which was. There is nothing left to conquer. Your song reaches the rubble. Gather the pieces to you like a mother waiting for the wind's frenzy to quiet.

Chapter 11:
[How to Greet the End]

When the wind brings a red pollen that covers every surface. When the wind makes the sound of a struggling star, knocks on the door of your throat. When the wind becomes a clock that counts down a cut, a cloud that captures a crow.

When the wind opens to a crater that creates a hole inside the ocean even water refuses. When the wind wallows inside its own waste, for a mouth for a mouth that never closes.

When the wind enters your home, that small hollow that holds the heft of history.

There is no leaving, no light switch to flip. There is no ladder to lower, no shutter to close, no shower to clean this.

The wind finds you crouching. Are you covering your hands to hold your desire to hide your eyes?

At least there is a wolf to watch you weep.

Chapter 12:
[How a Species Becomes Extinct]

There is no next life. What you wasted is spread before you like a coral reef. What is the last image you saw? Did you memorize it? That you can't see won't matter. That you're still human, even for only an hour. That you have hands that can no longer harm. In your dreams the same deer is still your shadow.

Chapter 13:
[How to Dream of the Last Ice Age]

Hands become too frostbitten to hurt. Weapons are covered with snow, forgotten, lost until spring when flowers grow into a new petaled white. A clean deep well to surrender. In the Last Ice Age meadows are so green they turn coral in the sun. Only the very old die, a deep fall into a quiet sleep, and once the ice has thawed they journey out to sea with orchids placed over their eyes.

Chapter 14:
[How to Find the Last Ice Age]

A bear will ask you for your burden. *What is in your right hand?* A just-birthed boulder. *What is in your left hand?* Whistle of lost leaf, feather rust of ravaged land. Even the stars die eventually. The entrance will appear as a trapdoor in a cloud, the sky scattering in all directions.

Chapter 15:
[How to Locate a Trapdoor]

No handle, no hinge. The trapdoor is etched in ice, little angular cloud floating away. Don't wait. Somewhere a key or rope to pull yourself through to a circling sea lined violet. If a ship waits, if its sails are set to lift. Prepare your body—particles disassembling into a final goodbye to this other world.

Chapter 16:
[How the Last Ice Age Appears]

[1]

The sea will be covered with thousands of ships, each carrying a new animal to land. For years the ships roam various bodies of water like ghosts. The horizon holds eight different freedoms and a single sun destined to erupt. The animals never dream of destruction and never die.

[2]

In one legend there is a key to unlock the new animals.

In another fifty-one great blue herons make nests in the hull of each ship.

In another sirens fill the sky in a bright sweep of red. A fire that can't be extinguished spreads across the sea.

In another any animal who enters the fire is never violent again.

[3]

Each morning the beaches are littered with seaflowers and Styrofoam spiraling through sand like miniature windmills. The coast is layered with muddled jellyfish and candy wrappers, cigarette butts and plastic bottles. And underneath the water, sea pigs, flashlight fish, feather stars and fishing nets, bottle caps and broken glass and plastic bags move like unmoored moonfish in a kaleidoscope of ancient slime.

[4]

When the ships go to sleep each night the current stops and the new animals close their eyes because they know how the lungs and heart are needed until they aren't and then the universe becomes a darkness so deep nothing can stop it.

[5]

Eventually there are moss-covered fields the color of sage. A forest grows like a single tunnel of branch and leaf moving across the land. Roots and vines erupt from the ground. Trees and ferns burrow into abandoned buildings until each wall and window is encased in green. Buried deep beneath, cities decompose to swamp.

[6]

Ladders grow from the ocean's floor, stars webbing the sky like seeds. The sun steals all it can each day. Sometimes flocks of strange birds fly past the ships, orange wings stretched across the horizon like burning lizards. From a distance, their red chests balloon to bright skin and nestled deep within a collection of waiting eggs.

[7]

The sky blooms to violet as a valley of green light rises from the water. The ocean continues to beat its enormous liquid heart.

NOTES

Three specific books helped me develop an ecopoetics informed by nature and survival: Richard E. Byrd's memoir *Alone: The Classic Polar Adventure* and the dystopian novels *The New Wilderness* by Diane Cook and *The End We Start From* by Megan Hunter. The poem "Days North of Me" borrows the term "weird weather" from Alice Bell's *Guardian* article, "Sixty years of climate change warnings: the signs that were missed (and ignored)."

ACKNOWLEDGMENTS

My thanks to the following journals where many of these poems first appeared in earlier versions or with different titles: *Anchor, Ghost Proposal, Horse Less Press, MassPoetry, Painted Bride Quarterly, Pangyrus, Pith Journal, Salamander, Small Po[r]tions, Timber, Tinderbox.* And to Letter [r] Press for publishing a chapbook version titled *Expedition Notes [1-4]*.

My deepest gratitude to Nathalie Handal for choosing this book, Peter Covino and everyone at Barrow Street Press for their guidance and support, and Joan Houlihan and Diana Khoi Nguyen for their generosity. I am indebted to my various poetry communities for following me through the long process of writing these poems: Talvikki Ansel, Brigitte Byrd, Amaranth Borsuk, Jessica Bozek, Nadia Colburn, Rosann Kozlowki, Lilly McCrea, Kevin McLellan, Anna Ross, Judi Silverman, and Cheryl Clark Vermeulen. I thank two ecopoetry workshops that provided me time and space to consider the natural world more deeply: Orchid Tierny's Liminal Lab workshop *Sensing Climate Hope: Ecopoetics and the Body*, and Elizabeth Bradfield's workshop *It Is Solved by Walking: An Eco-Poetry Workshop* at the Fine Arts Work Center; and the Colrain Poetry Manuscript Conference for encouraging me during a pivotal revision of the book. My love to Jeremy Blackowicz who always believes in my creative process and to my 5-year-old daughter, Serin, who is already trying to take good care of our earth.

Carrie Bennett is the author of three previous poetry collections, *biography of water*, *The Land Is a Painted Thing*, and *Lost Letters and Other Animals*. She holds an MFA from the Iowa Writers' Workshop and currently teaches writing at Boston University. She is a Massachusetts Cultural Council Artist Fellow and lives in Somerville, Massachusetts with her family.

BARROW STREET POETRY

The Mouth Is Also a Compass
Carrie Bennett 2024

Brutal Companion
Ruben Quesada 2024

Brother Nervosa
Ronald Palmer 2024

The Fire Road
Nicholas Yingling 2024

Close Red Water
Emma Aylor 2023

Fanling in October
Pui Ying Wong 2023

Landscape with Missing River
Joni Wallace 2023

Down Low and Lowdown...
Timothy Liu 2023

*the archive is all
in present tense*
Elizabeth Hoover 2022

Person, Perceived Girl
A.A. Vincent 2022

Frank Dark
Stephen Massimilla 2022

Liar
Jessica Cuello 2021

*On the Verge of Something Bright
and Good*
Derek Pollard 2021

*The Little Book of
No Consolation*
Becka Mara McKay 2021

Shoreditch
Miguel Murphy 2021

Hey Y'all Watch This
Chris Hayes 2020

Uses of My Body
Simone Savannah 2020

Vortex Street
Page Hill Starzinger 2020

*Exorcism Lessons
in the Heartland*
Cara Dees 2019

American Selfie
Curtis Bauer 2019

Hold Sway
Sally Ball 2019

Green Target
Tina Barr 2018

*Luminous Debris: New &
Selected Legerdemain*
Timothy Liu 2018

*We Step into the Sea: New and
Selected Poems*
Claudia Keelan 2018

Adorable Airport
Jacqueline Lyons 2018

Whiskey, X-ray, Yankee
Dara-Lyn Shrager 2018

For the Fire from the Straw
Heidi Lynn Nilsson 2017

Alma Almanac
Sarah Ann Winn 2017

A Dangling House
Maeve Kinkead 2017

Noon until Night
Richard Hoffman 2017

Kingdom Come Radio Show
Joni Wallace 2016

In Which I Play the Run Away
Rochelle Hurt 2016

*The Dear Remote
Nearness of You*
Danielle Legros Georges 2016

Detainee
Miguel Murphy 2016

*Our Emotions Get Carried Away
Beyond Us*
Danielle Cadena Deulen 2015

Radioland
Lesley Wheeler 2015

Tributary
Kevin McLellan 2015

Horse Medicine
Doug Anderson 2015

This Version of Earth
Soraya Shalforoosh 2014

Unions
Alfred Corn 2014

O, Heart
Claudia Keelan 2014

Last Psalm at Sea Level
Meg Day 2014

Vestigial
Page Hill Starzinger 2013

You Have to Laugh:
New + Selected Poems
Mairéad Byrne 2013

Wreck Me
Sally Ball 2013

Blight, Blight, Blight,
Ray of Hope
Frank Montesonti 2012

Self-evident
Scott Hightower 2012

Emblem
Richard Hoffman 2011

Mechanical Fireflies
Doug Ramspeck 2011

Warranty in Zulu
Matthew Gavin Frank 2010

Heterotopia
Lesley Wheeler 2010

This Noisy Egg
Nicole Walker 2010

Black Leapt In
Chris Forhan 2009

Boy with Flowers
Ely Shipley 2008

Gold Star Road
Richard Hoffman 2007

Hidden Sequel
Stan Sanvel Rubin 2006

Annus Mirabilis
Sally Ball 2005

A Hat on the Bed
Christine Scanlon 2004

Hiatus
Evelyn Reilly 2004

3.14159+
Lois Hirshkowitz 2004

Selah
Joshua Corey 2003